BACKSTREET BOYS
Backstage Pass
A Photo Scrapbook

by Lauren Alison

SCHOLASTIC INC.
New York Toronto London Auckland Sydney
Mexico City New Delhi Hong Kong

This unofficial scrapbook is not authorized by or affiliated with the Backstreet Boys, their management, or Jive Records.

Photo credits: front cover (left to right): Steve Granitz/Retna; Melanie Edwards/Retna; Melanie Edwards/Retna; Paul Bergen/Redferns/Retna; Paul Bergen/Redferns/Retna; **back cover** Justin Thomas/Retna

p. 3 APRF/Shooting Star; **p. 4** (top) Larry Busacca/Retna; (bottom) Janette Beckman/Retna; **p. 5** (top) Jesse Frohman/Outline; (bottom) Jesse Frohman/Outline; **p. 6** Ron Wolfson/London Features; **p. 7** Larry Busacca/Retna; **p. 8** Janet Macoska; **p. 9** (top) Janet Macoska; (bottom) Janet Macoska; **p. 10** Janet Macoska; **p. 11** (top) Janet Macoska; (bottom) Janet Macoska; **p. 12** (top) Janet Macoska; (center) Janet Macoska; (bottom) Janet Macoska; **p. 13** Fred Duval/Famous; **p. 14** (top) Janet Macoska; (bottom) Janet Macoska; **p. 15** (top) Janet Macoska; (center) Larry Busacca/Retna; (bottom) APRF/Shooting Star; **p. 16** Larry Busacca/ Retna; **p. 17** (top) Paul Bergen/Redferns/Retna; (bottom) Melanie Edwards/Retna; **p. 18** (top) Connie Brukin/Sterling McFadden; (bottom) Janet Macoska; **p. 19** (top) Janet Macoska; (center) Larry Busacca/Retna; (bottom) Ernie Paniccioli/Retna; **p. 20** Fred Duval/Famous; **p. 21** (top) Janet Macoska/Retna; (bottom) Janet Macoska; **p. 22** (top) Janet Macoska; (bottom) Janet Macoska; **p. 23** (top) Janet Macoska/Retna; (bottom right) Fred Duval/Famous; (bottom left) Frank Frenzi Forcino; **p. 24** Steve Granitz/Retna; **p. 25** (top) Deluze/Shooting Star; (bottom) Larry Busacca/Retna; **p. 26** Janet Macoska; **p. 27** (top) Justin Thomas/Retna; (bottom right) Janet Macoska; (bottom left) Janet Macoska; **p. 28** Larry Busacca/Retna; **p. 29** (top) Connie Brukin/Sterling McFadden; (bottom) Paul Bergen/Redferns/Retna; **p. 30** Janet Macoska; **p. 31** (top) Fred Duval/Famous; (center) Janet Macoska; (bottom) Ernie Paniccioli/Retna; **p. 32** Larry Busacca/Retna; **p. 33** (top) Janet Macoska/Retna; (bottom) Mick Hutson/Redferns/Retna; **p. 34** (top) Jeremy Bembaron/Sygma; (bottom) Jeremy Bembaron/Sygma; **p. 35** (top) Jeremy Bembaron/Sygma; (center) Janet Macoska; (bottom) Jeremy Bembaron/Sygma; **p. 36** (top)David Fisher/London Features; (bottom) Paul Fenton/Shooting Star; **p. 37** (top) Phil Loftus/Retna; (center) Fred Duval/Famous; (bottom) Jeff Slocomb/Outline; **p. 38** (top) Larry Busacca/Retna; (center) Larry Busacca/Retna; (bottom) Larry Busacca/Retna; **p. 39** (top) Ernie Paniccioli/Retna; (bottom) Ernie Paniccioli/Retna; **p. 40** (top) Janet Macoska; (bottom) Janet Macoska; **p. 41** (top right) Hubert Boesl/Famous; (top left) Hubert Boesl/Famous; (bottom) Hubert Boesl/Famous; **p. 42** (top) Pierre ZonZon/South Beach Photo; (bottom) Pierre ZonZon/South Beach Photo; **p. 43** (top) Pierre ZonZon/South Beach Photo; (center) Pierre ZonZon/South Beach Photo; (bottom) Pierre ZonZon/South Beach Photo; **p. 44** (top) Paul Bergen/Redferns/Retna; (bottom) Justin Thomas/Retna; **p. 45** Melanie Edwards/Retna; **p. 46** (top) APRF/Shooting Star; (bottom) Nick Van Ormondt/London Features; **p. 47** (top) Goedefroit Music/London Features; (bottom) Sebastian Dufour/Gamma; **p. 48** Edie Baskin/Outline

ISBN 0-439-04531-2

Designed by Ursula Herzog

12 11 10 9 8 7 6 5 4 3 2 1   8 9/9 0 1 2 3/0
Printed in the U.S.A.
First Scholastic printing, September 1998

BSB—
They've Got It Goin' On

A.J. Howie Kevin Brian Nick

Orlando, Florida. Home of Disney World, Universal Studios, and now . . .
the BACKSTREET BOYS!!

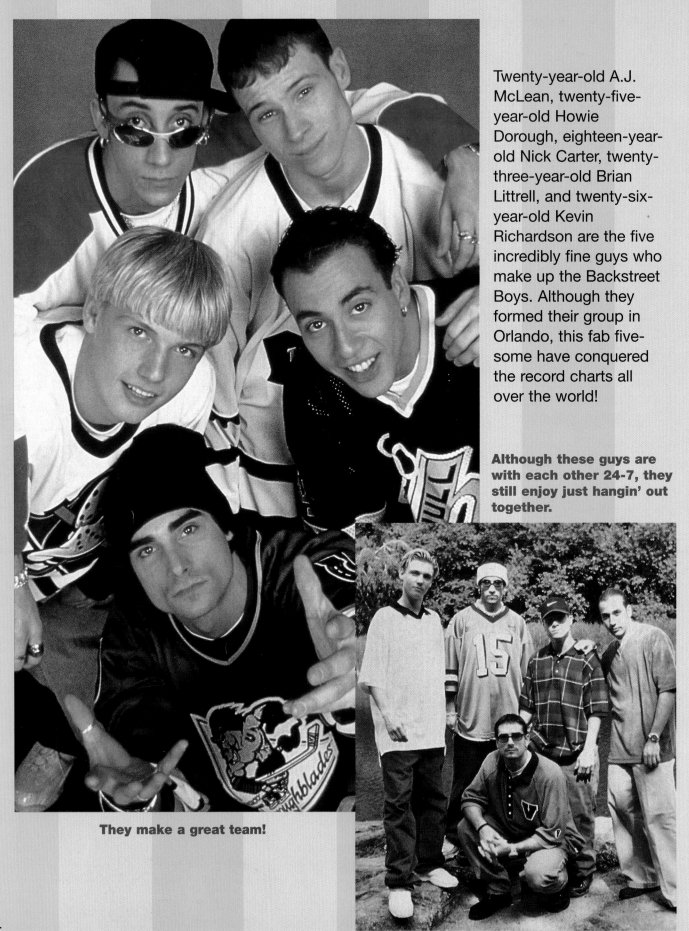

Twenty-year-old A.J. McLean, twenty-five-year-old Howie Dorough, eighteen-year-old Nick Carter, twenty-three-year-old Brian Littrell, and twenty-six-year-old Kevin Richardson are the five incredibly fine guys who make up the Backstreet Boys. Although they formed their group in Orlando, this fab five-some have conquered the record charts all over the world!

Although these guys are with each other 24-7, they still enjoy just hangin' out together.

They make a great team!

"We've been together every day for four years now. . . . It's like family. I never had a little brother, but now I've got four."
— Kevin Richardson (*USA Today*)

Kevin and his "little brothers" at play.

On set during a video shoot.

Backstreet Boys
Released UK: September 1996

We've Got It Goin' On / Anywhere for You / Get Down (You're the One for Me) / I'll Never Break Your Heart / Quit

Playing Games (With My Heart) / Boys Will Be Boys / Just to Be Close to You / I Wanna Be With You / Every Time I

Close My Eyes / Darlin' / Let's Have a Party / Roll With It /Nobody But You

Backstreet Boys
Released US: August 1997

We've Got It Goin' On / Quit Playing Games (With My Heart) / As Long As You Love Me / All I Have to Give /

Anywhere for You / Hey, Mr. DJ (Keep Playin' This Song) / I'll Never Break Your Heart / Darlin' / Get Down (You're the

One for Me) / Set Adrift on Memory Bliss / If You Want It to Be Good Girl (Get Yourself a Bad Boy)

Backstreet Boys "Enhanced Version"
Released US: 1997

We've Got It Goin' On / Quit Playing Games (With My Heart) / As Long As You Love Me / Everybody (Backstreet's Back)/

All I Have to Give / Anywhere for You / Hey, Mr. DJ (Keep Playin' This Song) / I'll Never Break Your Heart / Darlin' / Get

Down (You're the One for Me) / Set Adrift on Memory Bliss / If You Want It to Be Good Girl (Get Yourself a Bad Boy)

At a press conference at the All Star Cafe for the launch of their U.S. debut.

Singles (US)

•Quit Playing Games (With My Heart) •As Long As You Love Me •Everybody (Backstreet's Back) •All I Have to Give

Backstreet's Back
Released Europe & Canada

Everybody (Backstreet's Back) / As Long As You Love Me / All I Have to Give / That's the Way I Like It / 10,000

Promises / Like a Child / Hey, Mr. DJ (Keep Playin' This Song) / Set Adrift on Memory Bliss / That's What She Said /

If You Want It to Be Good Girl (Get Yourself a Bad Boy) / If I Don't Have You

BSB: The Beginning . . .

The Backstreet Boys' story is a tale of two cities. Actually, it's a *musical* tale of two cities.

City number one is Lexington, Kentucky, home of cousins Kevin Richardson and Brian Littrell. Both from musical families, the boys loved to harmonize everything from classic doo-wop hits, to barber shop quartet tunes, to music from Boyz II Men, Shai, and Jodeci. Even as little tykes, Brian and Kevin had it goin' on!

City number two is Orlando, Florida, where three local performers, A.J. McLean, Howie Dorough, and Nick Carter kept on bumping into each other at various auditions. They formed a singing group in the style of their favorite groups Boyz II Men and Color Me Badd.

Flashback to Lexington for a sec, where Kevin decided to leave the group he was performing with and go down to Orlando on a whim.

Back in the early days of BSB.

Kevin landed a job as a Disney World tour guide. One day, Kevin and a Disney World co-worker were on a break, talking about what they wanted to do with the rest of their lives. Kevin said he wanted to hook up with a singing group again, and his friend suggested he meet "these three guys who harmonize all the time."

When Kevin first heard A.J., Howie, and Nick's *a cappella* (without musical accompaniment) harmonies and saw their dance floor moves, he knew he had found a home, and the boys teamed up. But something was missing — a fifth voice. Enter Brian. Kevin called up his cousin (in fact he literally pulled him out of class!) and told him about the group he had just joined and invited him to come to Orlando to check it out. The very next day Brian headed to the airport and took off for Orlando . . . and eventual superstardom!

Could these guys be any closer?

Backstreet Boys — on the fast track to fame.

In the beginning: the Boys relaxing at Nick's house in October 1994.

BSB are hams for the cameras!

Thankfully, this "T-rex" spared the Boys!

In the studio, these five fine guys sing the sweetest of melodies.

BSB take a well-deserved break.

The Boys check out the production equipment.

Look at how sincere they are — these guys would never "play games with your heart"!

Meet the Boys!

Nick Carter

From the time he was a toddler, Nick was an entertainer. His family gladly tells tales of their baby boy, wearing only diapers, bustin' a move on the dance floor of the family club. "It was a lounge called the Yankee Rebel, which my father and Grandfather both owned — it was a small place," Nick recalled in an interview with *SuperTeen*.

In the fourth grade, the showbiz bug bit when Nick landed the lead in a production of *Phantom of the Opera*. He entered lots of talent shows, and remembers one in which he tried an impersonation of Elvis — leg shake and all! "I had to try," he told *Live & Kicking*. "I'm not really a dancer though. You gotta remember, I was really young when I started doing that stuff."

But he was doing something right and was soon the featured vocalist at the Tampa Bay Buccaneer pre-game shows.

Nick in the beginning of BSB — how adorable.

Even in the early days, Nick could bang out a beat!

14

This NFL gig lasted two years, and then when Nick was twelve, he won top prize on the 1992 *New Original Amateur Hour* TV show. Local commercial gigs came quickly after that, and Nick kept himself busy performing and auditioning at local Tampa and Orlando events. Even though he was only in junior high at that time, Nick made friends with two older guys he kept running into at the same gigs — A.J. McLean and Howie Dorough. The three started passing the long waits at auditions and performances by harmonizing together. And that was the birth of the Backstreet Boys!

Nick cooling off after an exhausting show.

He's *such* a hottie!

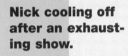

Drawing is one of Nick's secret talents.

Nick flashes a smile that makes us melt!

Serenading an adoring crowd.

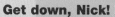

Get down, Nick!

Vital Stats:

Full Name: Nicholas Gene Carter
Nicknames: Nick, Nicky, Chaos
Birth Date: January 28, 1980
Zodiac Sign: Aquarius
Birthplace: Jamestown, New York
Current Residence: Tampa, Florida
Height: 6'
Shoe Size: 11
Hair: Blond
Eyes: Blue
Parents: Bob and Jane Carter
Sibs: Brother Bobbie Jean (B.J.);
Sister Lesley, and Twins Aaron and
Angel
Pets: A Persian cat named Muffy, a
Siamese cat named Blue Boy, and a
mixed cat named Bandit; a
Doberman named Conrad and a
golden retriever named Simba

FAVES:

Music: Alternative
Singer: Steve Perry
Musical Groups: Boyz II Men, Nirvana, Journey, Wu-Tang Clan
Food: Extra-cheese pizza
Ice Cream: Mint chocolate chip and chocolate chip cookie dough
Color: Green
School Subjects: Science, history, English, physical education
Sports: Water sports like scuba diving, football, horseback riding, basketball, baseball
Little Known Fact: Nick had a very small—"almost an extra"—role in the hit Johnny Depp movie, *Edward Scissorhands*.

Howie Dorough

When Howie was a kid, he was a major Michael Jackson fan. "Michael had a big influence on my life, in terms of inspiring me to sing," Howie told *BOP!* "He's a great artist, he's incredibly talented. When I was a little kid, I had the album *Thriller,* I had the Michael Jackson glove, and I even had the *Thriller* skateboard!"

Howie started performing when he was seven. "My first play was *The Wizard of Oz,*" Howie told *16* magazine. But that was just the beginning. Quickly, Howie got into the fast-track showbiz whirl. He performed in Orlando community theater productions, did a Nickelodeon pilot called *Welcome Freshman*, and appeared in the films *Parenthood* and *Cop and a Half.*

Howie knew that showbiz was going to be his life and he even earned an Associate of Arts degree in music. No wonder many consider him the backbone of BSB.

Howie flashes us those puppy dog eyes!

When Howie's not making his own music, he grooves to soul and R&B.

Howie chows on an omelette that Kevin whipped up at their apartment.

Gettin' serious for the camera.

At a press conference Howie lets us know that BSB love their fans!

Howie gives it his all whenever he's on stage.

Howie picks out his newest and coolest gear.

Howie and Tweety Bird say "cheese."

FAVES:
Singers: Jon Secada, Al B. Sure, Phillip Bailey
Musical Group: Boyz II Men
Ice Cream: Oreo Cookies and Cream
Color: Purple
School Subject: Math
Sports: Water sports like skiing and knee skiing, racquetball

A.J. McLean

A.J.'s very first acting job was when he was seven years old. He played Dopey in *Snow White and the Seven Dwarfs.* And he stole the show! "I was the main squeeze," A.J. told a Scholastic magazines writer. "All the girls thought I was really cute. And I went out and signed autographs for all the little kids. And it was funny — back then I signed my full name, because that's what I thought you were sup-posed to do. But now, I just write 'A.J.' because that's who I am."

By the time A.J. was in sixth grade, he had appeared in twenty-seven productions. And in junior high, he won a part on Nickelodeon's *Hi Honey, I'm Home.* During that time, A.J. took classes in dancing, singing, and acting — he knew what he wanted to do. Of course, it all clicked when he met up with Nick and Howie.

Did you know that A.J.'s a ventriloquist?

Welcome to A.J.'s house.

A.J. and his mom share a close bond.

Most of A.J.'s fans know he is very close to his mom, Denise. As a matter of fact, many of them have probably seen her and don't even know it! Denise began traveling with A.J. when he first started with the group, because he was under eighteen.

Before A.J. wanted to sing, he wanted to dance — now he thrills us with both talents!

A.J. at the San Remo Pop Festival.

Here's lookin' at you, A.J.

This pose is classic A.J.

Vital Stats:
Full Name: Alexander James McLean
Nicknames: A.J., Mr. Cool
Birth Date: January 9, 1978
Zodiac Sign: Capricorn
Birthplace: West Palm Beach, Florida
Current Residence: Kissimmee, Florida
Height: 5'9"
Hair: Brown
Eyes: Brown
Parents: Denise and Bob McLean (his parents were divorced when he was four years old)
Sibs: None
Pet: A dachshund named
 Tobi Wan Kenobi

A.J. sings his heart out!

FAVES:
Musical Groups: Blackstreet, Boyz II Men
Ice Cream: Vanilla with caramel topping, and mint chocolate chip
Colors: Yellow, and sometimes purple
School Subjects: English, history
Sports: Billiards, basketball, volleyball
Hobbies: Drawing cartoons, puppeteering

Brian Littrell

According to Howie, Brian is definitely the group funnyman! "He keeps us laughing," says Howie. The funny thing is that Brian's first exposure to music and performing was anything but on the light side. He spent his early years in Lexington, Kentucky, singing in his local church, and other regional churches, revivals, and even weddings.

Brian feels he has a lot to thank God for. You see, as a young child he was very ill and didn't even know it. "I was born with a heart murmur," he told *BOP!* "I have a hole in my heart and the doctors didn't know."

It wasn't until 1980, when Brian cracked his head on the sidewalk and was rushed to the hospital, that his parents found out that their boy was seriously ill. At the hospital, complications set in and Brian got a blood infection. "I had no chance of living

Brian charms everyone with his sweet smile.

26

A boy and his guitar — what a perfect pair.

Is Brian the next Michael Jordan? We don't think so.

whatsoever. The doctors were telling my mother and father to go ahead and make the funeral arrangements."

But then the unexpected happened — Brian surprised everyone and recovered!

However, in May 1998, it was announced that Brian would have to undergo heart surgery. But fans blew a big sigh of relief when Brian came through the surgery just fine. Brian requested that instead of cards and flowers, his well-wishers send donations to the Brian Littrell Fund for Pediatric Cardiology at St. Joseph Hospital in Lexington, Kentucky.

As of press time of this book, Brian was planning to join the Boys on their tour after he recuperated.

A guy who does his own laundry is all right with us!

With that look, Brian is simply irresistible!

Vital Stats:
Full Name: Brian Thomas Littrell
Nicknames: B-Rok, Seaver, Mr. Joker, B
Birth Date: February 20, 1975
Zodiac Sign: Pisces
Birthplace: Lexington, Kentucky
Current Residence: Orlando, Florida
Height: 5'7"
Hair: Dirty blond
Eyes: Blue
Parents: Jackie and Harold Littrell
Sibs: Older brother Harold
Pet: A cat named Missy

Brian is known as the "comedian" of BSB.

Brian is such the showman!

FAVES:
Singer/Producer: Babyface
Musical Groups: Boyz II Men, Jodeci
Food: Pizza, mac & cheese
Ice Cream: Plain vanilla with chocolate chips
Color: Midnight blue
School Subject: Math
Sports: Basketball, golf, swimming

Brian's secret confession: "I bite my fingernails — I've tried to stop but I can't. It bothers me because when I'm signing autographs, the girls are like, 'You bite your nails!'"

Kevin Richardson

Kevin spent the first nine years of his life on a ten acre farm in Harrisburg, Kentucky. And when his family left the farm, they moved into a real modern-day log cabin on the grounds of a summer camp/retreat.

"I had a great childhood," Kevin says in his Jive Records bio. "I loved school, played Little League football, rode horses and dirt bikes, and sang into a hairbrush in front of my bedroom mirror."

Kevin got his first set of keyboards when he was a high school freshman. He also joined the chorus and drama club in high school, where he got his first real taste of what it's like to be onstage.

"When you're onstage, you can see people's reactions and that is the greatest feeling of all," Kevin told *All-Stars* magazine. "That's why we're here. That's the natural high."

Kevin, back in the day.

30

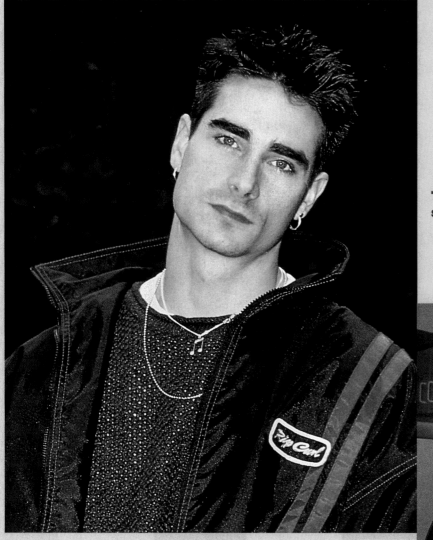

The words "tall, dark, and hand-some" seem to fit.

So cute — and he cooks too!!

Kevin ponders his response at a press conference.

Kevin, keepin' it real!

Kevin describes himself as "honest, sincere, and dedicated."

Vital Stats:
Full name: Kevin Scott Richardson
Nicknames: Kev, Kevi
Birth Date: October 3, 1972
Zodiac Sign: Libra
Birthplace: Lexington, Kentucky
Current Residence: Orlando, Florida
Height: 6'1"
Hair: Dark brown
Eyes: Green
Parents: Ann and Jerald Richardson Sr.
Sibs: Brothers Jerald and Tim
Pet: A cat named Quincy

FAVES:
Singers: D'Angelo, The Artist, Elton John, Billy Joel
Musical Group: The Eagles
Food: Mom's cooking! Also Mexican and Chinese
Colors: Black, blue
School Subjects: History, geometry
Sports: Football, surfing, rugby, horseback riding, swimming

"I'm a shy guy. Sometimes I think too much about what I'm going to say to somebody or what they are going to think." (*BOP!*)

Kevin is all about the music!

Backstreet Baby: Aaron Carter

There's a new kid on the block — ten-year-old Aaron Carter, the adorable little brother of Nick Carter. While big brother Nick's been touring with the Backstreet Boys, Aaron's been wowing audiences overseas. Aaron actually formed a band when he was seven, but soon decided to go solo. He currently has two huge hits overseas, "Crush on You" and "Crazy Little Party Girl," and released his first album, *Aaron Carter*, in the U.S. in June. And tons of fans got to check out Aaron in person when he opened for the Backstreet Boys on their 40-city tour that began in the summer of '98.

Aaron also filmed four videos. The first, *Crush on You,* was filmed in Los Angeles with bro Nick. Video number two, *Crazy Little Party Girl,* was filmed in Vancouver, BC, Canada. And numbers three and four, *I'm Gonna Miss You Forever* and *Shake It* were filmed in Florida.

Aaron takes after his big bro Nick.

Fine-tuning his guitar.

Aaron has a lot a fans — including Mickey Mouse!

Even though Aaron's a bit more rock-oriented than his big bro, they're both as cute as can be! And if you look at a picture of Nick from a few years ago, you might confuse him for Aaron!

For those of you who don't know Aaron real well, or who want to get more info on this little cutie, here's the scoop:

Aaron's tight with Nick and his other siblings.

Full Name: Aaron Charles Carter
Nickname: A.C. — BSB gave it to him in Germany!
Birth Date: December 7, 1987 (he has a twin sister Angel!)
Zodiac Sign: Sagittarius
Birthplace: Tampa, Florida
Current Residence: Ruskin, Florida
Pets: Cats Sugar, Bandit, Lucky; Dogs Simba, Salty, Pepper, Samson
Fave Singers: Backstreet Boys, 'N Sync, Tom Petty & the Heartbreakers
Fave Sport: Football
Fave Food: Pizza

Aaron bonds with his mom and twin sister, Angel — what a scream!

35

Nick, A.J., and Howie stand for the cameras at the 1998 World Music Awards.

Awards

In November 1996, the Backstreet Boys were voted Most Popular Band in Europe at the MTV European Music Awards, beating off stiff competition from Oasis, the Spice Girls, and Jamiroquai.

Also in '96, the Boys were voted Best International Group by German TV viewers. Their single "I'll Never Break Your Heart" went gold there, and topped the charts in Austria as well.

At the Smash Hits Awards, the Boys walked away with a whopping five awards: Best Album and Best Album Cover for *Backstreet's Back*, Best Video for "Everybody," Best International Band, and a special award to Nick for Best Male Haircut!

BSB are all smiles at the 1997 Billboard Awards.

A proud night for BSB at the European MTV Awards.

BSB sizzled at the Smash Hits Awards.

BSB looking oh-so-smooth for the 25th Annual American Music Awards.

BSB launches their U.S. debut with a performance at the Virgin Megastore in New York.

BSB U.S. Debut The Second Time Around!

The debut American CD, *Backstreet Boys,* had an August 12, 1997, release date. The first single from the CD — "Quit Playing Games (With My Heart)" — hit the radio stations on June 27. It debuted on *Billboard*'s "Hot 100 Singles" chart its first week as the Hot Shot Debut at number 24. Within two weeks it climbed to the number 2 spot and soon topped the charts.

But this wasn't the Backstreet Boys' *real* debut in the U.S. In 1995 they completed the single "We've Got It Goin' On," and it was released both in the United States and in Europe. Everyone impatiently awaited the weekly chart reports — only to be disappointed. "We've Got It Goin' On" only went to number 69 on *Billboard*'s top pop chart.

Why did they work the second time around? Well, maybe the time was just right for their infectious tunes!

Check out Howie! He was psyched for the BSB Virgin Megastore gig!

At a press conference for their U.S. debut at the All Star Cafe in New York.

Backstreet Boys at a private concert for winners of a radio contest in New York City.

"We finally have time to focus on our home-land. We got our start everywhere else, all over the world, except home, so it's time to just come back, relax a little bit, and focus on the U.S. fans."
—Brian Littrell (UPI)

Howie and Nick help out at "Christmas in April," a community service event in Cleveland, Ohio.

After the work was done, BSB rewarded the other volunteers with an impromptu melody.

All for One, One for All

BSB was thrilled to lend a hand to "The Big Help," a Nickelodeon benefit in Los Angeles.

Nick belting out a tune for a good cause.

Not only do the Boys support one another, they are also into helping out their community. Ever since they started, they've taken time from their hectic schedules to raise money and awareness for different causes. They actually pitched in at "Christmas in April," a community cleanup project in Cleveland, and they performed for Nickelodeon's "The Big Help" in Los Angeles. These guys are super willing to do whatever they can!

Backstreet Boys strut their stuff for the audience.

Every member of BSB was struck hard by the devastation of their home base, Orlando, Florida, after a series of tornadoes ravaged the area. They all wanted to help the people who were hit the hardest, so they were thrilled to participate in "Orlando Bands Together," a central Florida relief project. With lots of other ultra-cool bands, they made tons of money to go to the tornado victims. It was a spectacular concert and a mega-success!

Backstreet Boys love getting gifts from their fans.

These are from A.J. . . . to you!!

Howie, A.J., and Nick.
Forgive A.J., he gets a little *too* excited at times.

These guys
make helping
the community
fun!

Kevin fills out a
check donation
to benefit
tornado victims.

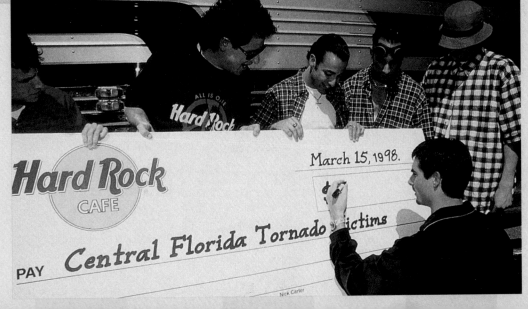

Hard Rock
CAFE

ALL IS ONE
Hard Rock

March 15, 1998.

PAY *Central Florida Tornado* victims

Nick Carter

Because their onstage choreography is so demanding, all of the Boys have been known to lose up to four and a half pounds each during a performance!

The Backstreet Boys kicked off their world tour on July 8 in Charlotte, North Carolina. Here's a look at their tour schedule as of press time:

Backstreet Boys performing at the San Remo Pop Festival.

DATES	CITIES
July 8, 1998	Charlotte, NC
July 9, 1998	Jacksonville, FL
July 10, 1998	Miami, FL
July 11, 1998	Orlando, FL
July 12, 1998	Atlanta, GA
July 15, 1998	Blistrow, VA
July 16, 1998	Philadelphia, PA
July 17, 1998	New York, NY
July 18, 1998	New Haven, CT
July 19, 1998	Albany, NY
July 21, 1998	Darien Lake, NY
July 22, 1998	Cleveland, OH
July 23, 1998	Fishers, IN
July 24, 1998	Detroit, MI
July 25, 1998	Louisville, KY
July 26, 1998	St. Louis, MO
July 28, 1998	Houston, TX
July 29, 1998	Dallas, TX
July 31, 1998	Kansas City, KS
August 1, 1998	Chicago, IL
August 2, 1998	Milwaukee, WI
August 4, 1998	Denver, CO
August 6, 1998	Salt Lake City, UT
August 7, 1998	Las Vegas, NV
August 8, 1998	Los Angeles, CA
August 11, 1998	San Francisco, CA
August 13, 1998	Portland, OR
August 15, 1998	Vancouver, BC, Canada

DATES	CITIES
August 18, 1998	Edmonton, Alberta, Canada
August 19, 1998	Saskatoon, Saskatchewan, Canada
August 20, 1998	Winnipeg, Manitoba, Canada
August 22, 1998	Toronto, Ontario, Canada
August 23, 1998	Montreal, Quebec, Canada
August 25, 1998	Halifax, Nova Scotia, Canada
August 27, 1998	Hempstead, NY
August 28, 1998	Scranton, PA
August 29, 1998	East Rutherford, NJ
August 31, 1998	Grand Essex, VT
September 1, 1998	Providence, RI
December 1, 1998	Köln, Germany
December 2, 1998	Münster, Germany
December 3, 1998	Berlin, Germany
December 4, 1998	Leipzig, Germany
December 5, 1998	Kassel, Germany
December 6, 1998	Mannheim, Germany
December 7, 1998	Zurich, Switzerland
December 9, 1998	Friedrichshafen, Germany
December 10, 1998	Weis, Germany
December 11, 1998	München, Germany
December 14, 1998	Hamburg, Germany
December 15, 1998	Frankfurt, Germany
December 16, 1998	Stuttgart, Germany
December 17, 1998	Bremen, Germany
December 18, 1998	Kiel, Germany
December 19, 1998	Essen, Germany
December 20, 1998	Köln, Germany

BSB On Stage

BSB always know how to wow the crowds with their hip performances!

The guys love the fab perks of fame — like traveling all around the world.

Cruising the canal in Amsterdam.

Backstage at a concert, the Boys like to have certain snacks — a vegetable plate with dip, cheese and crackers, apples, oranges, lemons, orange juice, bottled water, Coca-Cola, Orange Crush, and Grape Crush.

The Boys stare down the camera in concert.

What's Next?

Now that the Boys have conquered the entire world with their infectious grooves and perfect harmonies, what's next? Their fans are hoping for more, more, more! And that's what they'll get. The Boys will be on the road, and in the studio recording a new album. The Backstreet Boys are here to stay!